A Gentle Walk Through Nature

Denise L Gadreau

Aham Prema
I am Love

**In all of reality,
there is only Love!**

**Look no other
place but within.**

Table of Contents

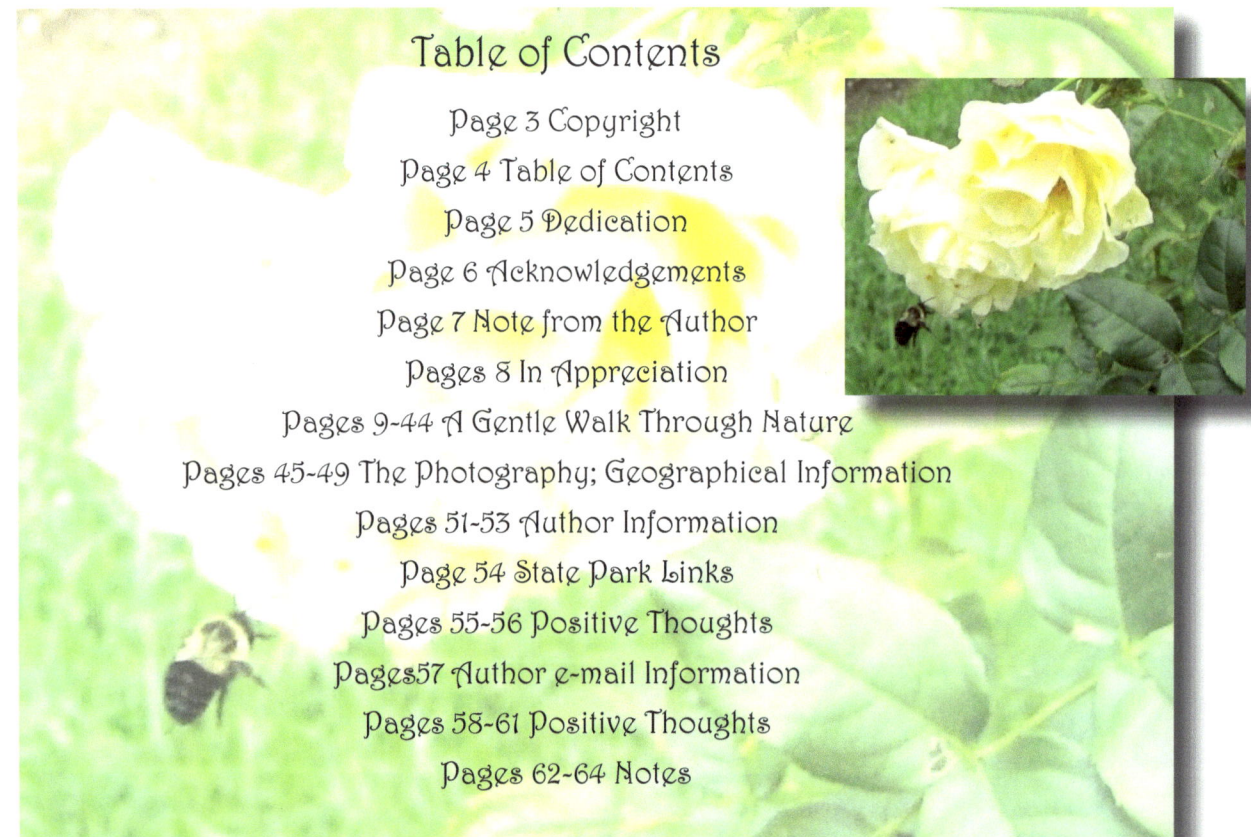

All Life can be intrinsically beautiful, even a little piece of nature can stimulate our senses. Can you feel with emotion the intensity of Love from the Mother's hand? She is guiding you to open your heart and your mind to the journey within. Rest in her gentleness

This book is dedicated
to all those who are in
love with Nature.

Author's Note

When I first thought about writing *A Gentle Walk Through Nature*, I had something completely different in mind. I considered going on the same format as one of my latest books, *Guided Visualizations for a Stress-Free Day*. Somehow the idea didn't resonate with me and I put if off for a few months.

One day I met with a friend and she gave me an idea as we were talking. So I decided to try it and the book took shape after that.

Many people are hurting, to what degree, sometimes we will never know. The goal of this book is to bring about a soothing atmosphere of calm and tranquility. Discovering comfort and healing in the arms of Nature, and the Divine, is to feel the love and bliss on a beautiful summer's day, such as this one the hiker has chosen in the book.

I hope through your journey, you find a restorative balm in *A Gentle Walk Through Nature*. May your walk through this book bring you Peace and Light.

Denise Gadreau

In Appreciation

Thank you Louise Leake for the idea you gave me that brought this book into existence.

Thank you Nat Wall, Kate Clark, Louise Leake, Cam and Mary Ann of Monday evenings for your unending friendship and the comradely we share.

I can never forget to show appreciation to Josh Downing, Louise Walkup and Cam Fogg and Carmen Gray for your continued support in my writing. Thank you with gratitude for your friendship. And Josh Downing who is my son, thank you for believing in me.

Thank you everyone who holds a special communion with Nature, and takes care of this beautiful Earth.

Thank you everyone who remembers Earth day every year and gives back to the Earth with love.

A Gentle Walk Through Nature

The early morning light streamed through the window creating cascades of iridescent dust particles dancing to the rhythm of sound not yet in existence. Sleeping dramas continue only within the ambiance of the dreamer, the fruition of sound only within the absence of consciousness.

It was an ordinary day, yet a day not yet cataloged within the awareness of the dreamer. Sonatas of light splayed around the vitality of this dimension, nimble at first, then as the morning progressed into dazzling warmth greeted by those fortunate enough to experience its splendor.

The dreamer slowly awakens, transcending all that she has experienced in her slumber state into the illusion of the reality created for this day, her day. A day she has chosen, aware and occasionally not aware of what she will notice. Sometimes awareness is not conscious until a drama sets in. Perhaps she will discover something new to think about; perhaps an epiphany will arise within her realizations of what unfolds today.

Slowly, looking around from the comfort of her bed, she spies the dust particles dancing their grandeur. She is spellbound for the moment, something she remembers within the

framework of her memory, but not quite placing it into existence. After a fleeting moment she throws back her covers and turns toward the window and looks through the laced curtains. Her feet in conjunction with the warm sunlit flooring, slowly sashays to the open window. A spider's web catches her eye, intricate and delicate artwork, interlacing to the far corner of the window pane. Curiosity lingers for a fraction of a second as she investigates each fragile strand of the network that glistens boldly in the sun. Her eyes now following the light that dances on the dewdrops, caresses onward to the drooping roses from the recent rain.

Petite pink blooms are transfixed into the tall grasses; she may not have noticed them except for the slight breeze rustling playfully around them. Her breath held for a moment, bleeding hearts she recalls as she sadly quietly exhales, assimilating the meaning into her own life.

Stretching her body to awaken fully, she misses the divine enchantment this interlude brings. A time of healing from the early morning intervention is overlooked. She looks, but feels nothing. She senses, but not joy.

In the outer realm of the forest trees, birds chirp away. Their quick little chattering can be heard from near and beyond, giving her a slow smile across her face, but not her heart. Her heart is heavy, and she cannot see or feel beyond its heaviness. She can hear the song of a mourning dove. With the melody so clear, so distinct, so inviting, she feels attuned with its soulful song. It reaches inside her, inside her whole being, as she quells the augury mystique it brings. Time has lapsed for a few minutes and as she brings herself around, makes an impulsive decision.

A rucksack is carefully packed. She cautiously places a pad and pencil, fruit and seed for the excursion. A sandwich and a flask of tea in case she is out longer than she intends to be. It will be a warm day; perhaps she could sit by the pond of flowers, relax a bit and take in the warm sun for a while. The imagery still yet to discover and formulate in her mind, waits in expectation. It is all up to her and for her to identify.

Placing her right hand on the door knob, she turns remembering one last item she forgot. She opens the middle draw of her desk, takes out a small velvet bag, and places it in her jeans pocket. Out of the corner of her eye, a fluttering movement passes by outside her window. A swallowtail butterfly skillfully lands on a white petal of a dogwood tree. This is a sign, she muses as she turns to let herself out of her front door. The sun is a little higher now; and sitting on a branch of a tree above her, she hears the gentle cooing of two doves welcoming her.

She lets herself out of the gate. The warm air feels distinct and tantalizing. As she approaches the pond, the stillness of it intrigues her mind's eye. The imageries within the ponds' reflections are so still, yet appear magically dimensional. All is tranquil in this realm of beginnings. A beginning of a simple and complex journey, the visionary walks on. Simplistic and multifaceted in nature she feels a kindred spirit here. The doves hovering before her have landed. Two beautiful light brown beings edge her toward a forest path.

16

The sunlight dapples through the leaves as a gentle wind's soothing caresses touch lightly upon her cheeks. She is slowly feeling more alive. She breathes deeply of this earthen place, the richness of the deciduous life waiting to greet her, inviting her to feel its love, to feel oneness here.

Her heart is still opaque, heavy with her thoughts as she ventures on. It is beautiful here, a gorgeous morning, she reflects, and smiles as a rabbit crosses her path and watches her from under the brush.

Approaching an old stone wall, she redirects a passing thought, not letting it come into completion, sighs inwardly and sits down. The wall is lopsided. She finds a comfortable spot and closes her eyes. All is calm and peaceful here. She hugs her knees and rests her head on them, and listens.

She listens to the silence, and within that silence is an acquaintance long forgotten. Something had been lost inside herself and she has wandered aimlessly, not knowing how to retouch that part which she has so desperately wanted to find. Wondering if she ever will, she continues to listen to the stillness around her.

Relaxing in the warm sun, hearing the sound of the bumble bees, brings pleasure to her now. She is lost in the recollection of sitting with her mother in her garden of flowers. The rich colors of the iris florae or the heady smell of the roses or lilacs when in bloom were always so alluring and uplifting.

She opens her eyes and spies a fat bumblebee curiously looking at her. He is wistfully considering her as a flower, but decides she isn't and brambles on to the next candidates near the wall. Again she smiles, but her heart doesn't resonate inside of her. It just is.

The forward motion of a breeze entices her and it is time to move on. Startled out of her reverie, she jumps from the wall, careful not to trample any of the flowers, and walks toward the direction of a small spring fed lake further on. She walks until she comes to a small marshy clearing, and just off the path, five minutes or so is the gem of what she seeks.

The sun, higher in the sky, reflects the clouds on the glass-blue water she journeys to. Studying its reflection, feels the picturesque postcard of this reserve. The breeze ripples on the water and she can barely hear it's sensation along the small threadbare shore occupied by brush and leaning trees. She hears something nearby. A movement catches her peripheral vision. A petite turtle swims along, oblivious of being an attraction in this extraordinary hideaway.

She watches for a while, time stretching for infinity, feeling illimitable, like a daydream come to pass. Sensitivity for the love of nature arises within her as its beauty sketches on and on. She inhales the fresh air and drinks in the splendor of the lake. Peaceful, so peaceful. A blue heron lands on the adjacent left, standing still in the water. She is broken out of her reverie, and adjusts her rucksack. The graceful heron finds its dinner, and flies off to another part of the lake.

She is about to move on but notices to the right side of the shoreline, just under the trees, a deer fawn quietly drinking the water. Its grace like body looks up, then around, spotting its mother, slowly dips its head down for another mouthful of cool refreshing water. The mother surveys the area and has spotted the watcher. Both are motionless, until the mother decides it is safe and drinks from the lake in turn.

Altering the rucksack on her shoulder, she realizes almost to the right of her location, a beautiful heart opening above her in the trees. Feeling the warmth about her, she looks over to the left and notices clouds forming a heart just above the trees.

The grass is lush near the shore, and she finds a place to sit comfortably. Unfastening her rucksack, she takes out the pad and pencil, and begins to write about the day so far. When she comes to the part about the heart formation of the branches in the trees and clouds, she writes; "I have always believed in Angels and maybe an Angel is sending me a message of love...."

Putting away the pad and pencil, she takes out an apple and some of the seed for the mourning doves not far from her. She eats her apple in quiet solitude listening to the sounds of Nature and the cooing of the doves.

After an interval, in the sanctuary of this environment, a soft pull of diversity resuscitates her ties of oneness that invited her. In the opening, she feels the pull, but unwarily eases herself out of it as she readies her journey back to the path.

She approaches the marshy area, reviewing the variance of the blue-glass water, to the stunning mirror at the wetland. A statuesque tree in the middle of the marsh seems to have weathered its old age and is set as a permanent marker for all to witness. The Guardian of this area in full regalia bids the seeker welcome. On this gorgeous day, the seeker views it's elegance with a slight nod of appreciation as she tarries for the time being, and then ventures her way back to the path.

Not far from the lake of glass is a steady walk to a set of cliffs that overlook a pond. She takes her time, paces the arduous climb and is amazed the doves are still around her. Feeling their comfort of companionship, she passes a watery area of purple aquatic flowers, and begins to feel the heat of the day. It feels so good, a warm sunny day, much like a day not too long ago. A reoccurring daydream has forced itself to the surface of her memory. Unaware of its impact, tears slowing fall as she stands for a while until she remembers where she is and slowly continues on. Walking and climbing a great distance, she can still hear the soft cooing of her companions near her. Continuing on the path, she feels a haven by their sounds and finds an opening for the first cliff. How blue the water is. A gentle breeze cools her from the warmth. She wanders closer to the rock protruding out over the pond, and settles down on a flat area under the protection of the trees.

The doves come closer. The two are together with their melodious sounds that echo in the distance off the cliff. They make her laugh as they tilt their heads curiously at her.

After a while, the peacemakers follow her as she stands and gingerly walks to the other side of the overhang, and down below, it is in shadow. Regarding the small stream coming from the edge of the pond, the water in whirlpool captured between the rocks, brings character to the moment. Such a difference here, like night and day she envisions.

On the cliff in-between the brush looking in, purple hydrangeas and orange pert lilies cascade through. They are uncultivated and she has always wondered how they grew in this wild woodland area. It is a stunning view from here and beyond.

A few days ago, she took a ride to a habitation with another glass like body of water. It was midafternoon and had been raining torrential downpours the day before. The stream on the other side of the swimming area was swollen and full to capacity. It was cloudy and not much sun and warmth for the middle of the summer. But when she crossed over to the swimming area, the sun came out and gave her a captivating gift, warmth and the vivid exquisiteness within the water. Her sandals off, she walked thoughtfully along the edge of the small shore.

30

The healing within her soul was lost to her as she sauntered on in silence dismissing the slightest chance of renewal. Her awareness was visionless. It was as if she were watching herself through another's eyes, with another's experience, with her breath bringing back to her own consciousness of realization as part of this earth, yet feeling nonexistent within it.

It is how she felt now, on the cliff within the shadow of the pond gazing at the hydrangeas and lilies. Existing, yet not fully being in the present moment. As if she lost part of herself somewhere without the knowledge of how to get it back, or if she ever could. It was unsettling and tiring when she deliberated about it. It wasn't anything she could talk about. When she tried to, no one seemed to understand what she was talking about.

But she did. She knew it was true.

Placing the rucksack back on her shoulders, she starts to think about the journey home. It is early afternoon. The doves make their subtle appearance along the edge of the path on the cliffs. Though the climb was strenuous, she finds it much easier to descend.

She decides to walk the long way home, keeping pace with her faithful companions, edges her way down the steep inclines. When she comes to a fork in the path, she is not sure which one to take. Both are very well known to her, both would get her home in due time.

The doves fly ahead of her and land on the right of the fork. Their gentle sounds beckon her to follow. "Well, you have decided for me," she says and follows them with confidence.

Forty-five minutes into the path, she walks with anticipation past borders of manicured shrubbery, and notices a small crowd gathered to observe a section of lotus flowers in bloom. Hundreds of flowers have risen to show their grandeur. They are so magnificent, she thinks. She enjoys the splendid beauty the petals give from the rays of the sun.

Feeling happy now, she witnesses the amicable joy that is present and shared among the crowd. A feeling of harmony has shifted her emotions. A guide talks to a group of women about how the flowers are endangered and signals to a sign posted prohibiting the flowers to be picked. The guide answers questions and talks about the history of the lotus flowers and how they came to be in the area now.

As she listens to the group lecture, she reflects how unfortunate it would be coming again next year and seeing fewer flowers in bloom if the general public were allowed to pick the delicate flowers.

The guide takes the group to another part of the forest. For that is where they are, on the far edge of a State Forest, near the walking trails to find Swallowtail Butterflies located in the conifers. Someone has spotted one and the group is walking around the bend, laughing and talking until they are out of sight.

Taking one last look at the lotus, she walks to another trail that will take her home.

Her gait a little lighter, she walks for some time until approaching a stream. Soft spongy grass edges its borders. It looks so inviting.

She has come to a magical place
filled with a faint rainbow of light,
and senses the harmony here.

Expressing delight, she makes herself comfortable, careful not to damage the few mushrooms sharing her space. It was an early morning for her and suddenly feels a little weary.

She places her rucksack down and rests her head on it. She can feel the lush grasses beneath her body and watches the water flowing over the moss-covered rocks. It is a soothing sound. The sunlight creates rainbows of color dancing on the water, and after a while mesmerizes her into a light daydream state.

Feeling the comfort of sound the water makes, she feels a tonal vibration coming from within the earth. She is aware of two beings near her. Two beautiful Angelic Beings that have dove like eyes. They are the eyes of kindness and compassion. She is comforted by their peaceful nature. In her dreamlike state, she is aware of the two beings watching over her.

Both presences smile down at her with such merriment. Iridescent colors glow all around them. They are radiant. Just being there with her fills her with immense joy. A joy she hasn't felt for a few years. She knows they are the cause of the sound toning of the earth. A vibrational sound starts to fill her whole being. She hears within her thoughts; "Are you willing to let go of all your suffering, to let go of the past? Are you willing to forgive and ready to live the destiny intended for you?"

She feels they are looking into her very soul, and suddenly desires a change. Too long has she wasted her time and life. She seeks healing now, movement toward the connection she has lost. "Yes'" she answers.

She hears the song of the Ancestors around her. The melodious far off song settled into the earth lifts up its Divine Song and encompasses her whole existence. Its Presence lifts its voice in tune with its inhabitants. It became her existence, this manifestation within the sphere of Nature, a sphere of healing and peace. Calm settles over her. One of the Angelic Beings touches her forehead. She feels the energy from the light reflecting on the slow steady water cleansing her body, and clearing her mind. Washing away her fears, healing every cell in harmony to the light, the beings quietly and compassionately wait.

She could feel the suffering in her heart melt into the terrain to be recycled into the earth. She as a connection to herself, had been lost through time, now through the very connection to Nature, reconnects to herself. How wonderful it feels, she expresses to herself and the two compassionate beings.

She hears, "Do you not know that you are Nature. Nature is not something separate from you. As you begin to reconnect to Nature, you begin to reconnect to yourself. Feel the Love of the Divine. She speaks to you through your love of Nature. Feel the Mother's presence, and you will feel healing within, for she is Divine Love."

The other Angelic Being touches her third eye area. She feels a whoosh of sound, a feeling of release going through her chakras. She can feel the healing and the joy enveloping inside of her. She is willing to let go all that has troubled her. She is willing to forgive. She accepts the healing and the joy.

The radiant Angelic Beings urge her to rest for a while. When she awakes, they are gone. All she sees are the two doves who have faithfully accompanied her to the mossy stream area. She stretches her arms and legs and sits up. She feels different. Her whole body feels lighter, as if a weight has been lifted. Looking around and appreciating her surroundings, she feels free. Free of her heavy heart she has carried around for so long.

Taking the little pouch out of her pocket, she releases the knot and takes out a beautiful celestite crystal. It glistens in the sun. Her two devoted companions cooing and waiting in expectancy watch her give thanks to her reconnection to Nature and to herself. Thanking the Divine, she drops the celestite into the flowing stream as a token of her love and for her healing. The doves fly around her cooing. Laughing, she feels refreshed and renewed, and full of life.

"Thank you my two friends," she waves as they fly down the path a little ways, waiting for her to collect her rucksack to walk the journey home.

Nightfall was already settling in as the evening progressed. She sat down to have a cup of tea. Taking out her notebook from her rucksack, she wrote down all that had happened by the iridescent stream. She wanted to remember every detail, so it could be read again every so often. She thought of the calming emotions rereading her experience would bring. It made her feel tingly with joy inside when she thought about it.

Turning from her writing, she notices a brilliant moon rising. Mother Nature was at its peak for the evening. She always admired a full moon over the water. How marvelous she thought.

Closing her notebook, she feels renewed and ready to face a new day in the morning.

Lingering into the evening, she is content. All is well.

"All is well," she thought with a smile.

She felt loved by the Divine. She knew there may be days of discouragement and disappointments, but now she truly understood that she is never really alone, and this made all the difference to her.

The Photographs

The Photographs

The Photographs

Page(s) 31~ Hydrangeas,
A Residence in Norwich, CT
32~Orange Lily, Griswold roadside, CT
33~Hedges at Mashamoquet Brook State Park,
Pomfret, CT
34-35 ~ Lotus Flowers, Roadside, Route 102,
Wickford RI
36~Swallowtail Butterfly, in Conifers ~
along roadside of Scotland, CT
37~Rainbow of colors in brook at the beginning of
trails ~ Old Furnace State Park Trail to Ross's Cliffs,
Killingly, CT
38~On the trail ~ Beach Pond, Exeter, RI
39~Little retreat pond at Cat Hollow Park~
Near dam in Dayville, CT
40~Purple Flowers, A Residence in Ledyard, CT
41-42~Pine Acres Campground,
Near the Lake, Salem, CT

The Photographs

Everyday is an Opportunity for a Miracle....

57~ Mohegan State Parks, Rose Garden
Flowers
58~Gardner Lake Boat Ramp, Salem, CT
59~ East Killingly Pond Road State
Reserve,
Killingly, CT
60~ Bigelow State Park,
Nipmuck Forest,
Union/Woodstock, CT
61~Route 164, Pachaug Lake,
Griswold, CT
62-64 East Killingly Pond Road State
Reserve,
Killingly, CT
65~ Mohegan State Parks, Rose Garden
Flowers

49

Denise Gadreau is the Author of various articles and eight books.

"Crystal Meditations, The Inward Journey," takes you through guided meditations with the use of crystals and common stones. With today's busy schedule and on the go lifestyle, learn to de-stress and go within for release and relief.

"Points of Light, A Poetic Journey," is a poetic journey of love, spiritual, and relative living; words of passion and healing. Through this book, you will feel the love for the earth, within yourself as you visualize and feel it extracted from the vivid adventure of words into something beautiful and alive.

"The Miracle is You, Life's Journey" is a series of articles to relieve stress, beautifully written and to the point.

"Light Wisdom, A Journey of Positive Quotes," is a photographic masterpiece. She includes her talent for artistic design with the pages of her positive quotes and affirmations. The photos and links of Trails & State Forests, brooks and floral are included in the last 10 pages.

The Reflections of the Norwich State Mental Hospital, 2008-2010, is a joint publication, in which she is a co-author. The book includes many photos of the deterioration of a once thriving era of 1904 through 1996 when it was finally closed.

Her fiction publication is quite different from her previous non-fiction genre. Here is a brief synopsis of her recent title: "The Epic Catalog."

Jeffery Turner is a man who does not realize he is from a parallel world. He is about to embark on a voyage to the Bahamas from England in the 1950's and meets an extraordinary stranger who sets the mystery in motion.

The Epic Catalog" is the title of this science fiction, mystery adventure. As the story develops, two 14 year old cousins, Anna and Desmond, find out about a book which Jeffery Turner has given account of. It is a tale that dates back from the 1950's to 2011, and as the two cousins read the book on the computer, they somehow find themselves part of the mystery.

Additional characters are an entomologist and his wife, an archaeologist, school teachers, a perpetual student with seven degrees, an antiques dealer, a plane taxi service, a museum professor and Mrs. Perpecuwitz who owns a summer attraction called Rose Cottage.

There are dimensional twists and turns, plane encounters with a UFO, a rescue at sea, open portals, Flyers known as Fairies in our dimensional world, and a surprise conclusion with a sequel in the future.

"Guided Visualizations for a Stress-Free Day," was designed for those who wish to release a little stress during their busy day or work week. The Photographs, visualizations, quotes and intuitive affirmations will help you unwind for as little as five minutes a day. This book is perfect for offices, teacher's lounges or a coffee table at home.

"A Photographic Journey, A Book of Days," will rekindle a viewer's fascination that Nature holds for all ages in the beauty, rest, peace, and relaxation of the photographs and special messages of encouragement and positive thinking. This book is in calendar form.

Web Page of various articles:
 http://renememlight.wordpress.com/

For Rhode Island Parks & Forests

http://www.riparks.com/Locations/LocationBeachPond.html

http://www.riparks.com/

For Connecticut Parks & Forests

http://www.ct.gov/deep/site/default.asp

~ Click on Parks & Forests
~ Click on: Select a State Park or Forest for Connecticut Parks & Forests.

http://www.empoweringparks.com/Connecticut.html

Every morning brings us new possiblities to make positive choices in our lives.

Perfect Balance brings order to Chaos. We need both to live in this world. When you think of volcanos that create mountains, disharmony bringing harmony, and physical seasonal changes in Nature bringing beauty & light. The autumn months and winter not long behind give us reflective options within our own selves as well as the whole world. We are really all one....

I hope your visual journey was one of peace and tranquility.

Please e-mail me at: dgadreau@live.com if you have any questions or would like to send me a note. I would love to hear from you.

I am on Facebook, if you have any comments. You can also leave a review on my Author's page on Amazon.com.

Many Blessings!

When we are truly awakened, what we have passed by will become enhanced, and truly beautiful.

In the midst of Nature, there goes my heart. The silence I welcome brings my mind into peaceful serenades of love for Mother Earth, I enter into the Nature of Bliss...

59

As you walk into this haven of Nature, you will indeed find peace and calm for your beautiful souls.

60

Every day there is living proof of a reality beyond words
that moves my existence into raptured harmony...

Nature exhibits much Love, in which we share so divinely.

Notes

Notes

Notes

This book, *A Gentle Walk Through Nature* was published in March, just before the Spring Equinox.

May this day for you be filled with Many Blessings!

www.ingramcontent.com/pod-product-compliance
Lightning Source LLC
Chambersburg PA
CBHW041503280526

45792CB00004B/1120